FROM THE HEART

One Hundred And One Palpitations

By:

John Harris Jr.

INTRODUCTION

These poems were written for me to express myself, free my mind and spiritually escape the bonds of social, economic and psychological captivity. To convey obstructions of justice, oppression, persecution, degradation, domination and discrimination. Relieve stress, reveal the contemplation and acquisition of affection and intimacy. A lot of them were also written by special request. Composed by design specifically for others own personal situations, desires, requirements, circumstances and specifications. To address their particular individual subject matter regarding wives, sweethearts, companions, immediate family members, friends, associates, and or acquainances. Now that you know the story behind it, read the book.
Enjoy!

#1
"ART FORM"

There are all kinds of art forms,
the best are those that do not conform to the
norm. There are the obvious ones,
painting, sculpture and such,
many people appreciate these very much.
But it doesn't stop here,
there is a wide range of art,
A lot of these, set themselves apart.
Like dance, music, theater too,
all of which, are art forms people can do.
Landscaping, architecture, and clothing
design, are all art forms that come to mind.
Writing is like painting with
alphabets, and when it comes to writing,
poetry is as good as it gets. For the record,
to any of you who don't buy this,
please remember,
I am bias.

#2
"FEELINGS"

You feel hot, you feel cold, you feel young, you feel old. How you feel, changes from moment to moment, and from day to day, but what factors are involved, to make you feel a certain way? They are external, internal, emotional, mental, and physical too, these are all influences, that make you feel the way you do. You feel love, you feel joy, you feel anger, you feel hate, some of which, can be changed, by things you take. So when you are feeling down and out, try to be calm, cool and collective, hopefully then, you won't just scream and shout.

#3
"TOUCH THE SOUL"

Some people just have that way of making you have a wonderful day. No matter how

sad or sick you may be, they can lift your spirits and set them free. It's just amazing to see,
how sweet they can be, whenever they come
around you see. How fantastic it is to see a
smile on their face, a beacon in the night, in a
dismal place. The way they talk, so calm and
soothing, as if to touch the soul, it is really
moving. Please, whoever you may be, never
give up that way you have of being sweet,
continue to do this, with whomever you meet.

#4

"IN DISTRESS"

What most people dream of is more or less the
same. Good health, prosperity, and happiness,
is the name of the game. Wishes and prayers
don't always come true, and it really doesn't
matter what you do. If something is meant, it
will come to be, whatever comes to pass, is

history. You can't change what happens, even in despair, you just have to put your best foot forward, and do it with care. In this world, a lot of people are without, I can understand, if they are sad, mad, pout and shout. They are tired of living in distress, when so many others, are blessed with the best.

#5
"EXCEPTIONAL ABILITY"

There are those who are just uncanny to me. These are the ones we refer to as a prodigy. They have a gift to do something effortlessly. It comes without trying, there is no denying, yes, it could give others a complex, with a skill beyond belief, good grief, are you for real, still it has a certain appeal. It is amazing to see, at least it is for me, how naturally, they, can display, such an exceptional ability.

#6
"HEART ENOUGH"

Please let me stress these facts, this situation won't let me relax. You are heavy on my mind, I think about you all of the time. Day and night, when I eat, when I sleep, when I'm alone in secret, I weep. Shedding a tear or two doesn't make me weak. It takes a strong man to have heart enough to cry, these waters flow for you, in case you wonder why. But things will be different, from here on out, of this fact, please have no doubt. From now on, I am a changed man, and we will soon be walking the aisle, hand in hand.

#7
"BY DESIGN"

Nothing in this world just happens by
chance, we are all victims of circumstance.
Everything you see is how it was meant to be.
We are a part of a grand design, even this
heart of mine. It's not only its physical valves
and chutes, but also its emotional
attributes. Somewhere, someone, devised a
scheme, and poof, then they dropped you on
the scene. I thought my heart would pop out
of my chest, now history will tell the
rest. Because I plan to spend my future with
you and that is all, by design too.

#8
"I LOVE YOU SO"

How do I show you my dear, the way I feel about you from year to year. The things you do, the words you say, the gleam in your eyes, when you look my way. You smell so sweet, all of the time, just a mere whiff of your fragrance, blows my mind. Your smile, so right, it could bring a black hole to light. The walk you have, takes my breath away, I swear before God, I come to love everything about you, more and more every day. The thought of living my life without you, is my greatest fear, I will always do whatever it takes, to keep you near. Finally, let me say, I pray, from the bottom of my heart, may we never, ever, be apart.

#9
"I'M THANKFUL"

Dear Heavenly Father, it is my understanding that I am not only suppose to be thankful for the blessings, but the trials and tribulations too. For no one knows the reasons why you do the things you do. So this is to give you recognition for what is good and bad and to tell you I'm grateful for all the things I've had. To let you know I appreciate all you send my way, from the sunny skies of summer, to when blue skies turn gray. I hope that this encompasses, all there is to be, and today you can realize, the gratitude in me.

#10
"FIRST CONTACT"

Once upon a time, I met someone very special to me, she made me feel the world was real, not just a fictitious fantasy. A dream come true, a fact of life, the caliber of woman, you call your wife. Although this may not be, the case just yet, it is something to consider, and attempt without regret. Until then, my very special friend, only time will tell, if it will come to that. In the meantime, I am very grateful, for the day, we made first contact.

#11
"MISS YOU MUCH"

The way you smell, the way you smile, I love your form, I love your style. The things you *say, when you talk, the way you sway, when you walk. The way you feel, when you touch, for all these reasons, I miss you much. Please believe me, when I say, I miss you much, in every way. So keep in mind, when you think of me, I'm out of mine, until you I see. When you sleep tonight, think of this, you are the one, I truly miss.*

#12
"A REMINDER"

I was just passing time, so I thought I would let you know, that you were on my mind. But that's nothing new, considering the special way, I feel about you. Still, I believe, you should, now and then, tell that special someone, what an affectionate mood they put you in. We sometimes get so busy, because life can put you in such a tizzy, that we can, for a while, forget the things, that make us smile.

Like that special someone, you hold so dear to your heart, and dread any time, that life keeps you apart. So here's a reminder for you to confer, anytime doubts of my feelings for you, suddenly occur.

#13

"WHEN I'M HOME"

Hello sweetheart, how are you today, please take care of yourself, while I'm away. I will be so glad when I am home again, holding you in my arms, kissing, hugging, and then, tell you how special you are to me, how glad I am that you and I became we. Yes time flies when you're having fun, but it goes so slow when you are away from the one, that makes your heart soar, like it has wings of its own, so let me tell you again, I will be glad when I'm home.

#14
"PUTTY IN YOUR HAND"

Had you on my mind, so I thought I would take the time, to drop you a line. Checking in, on a special friend, just to say, how are you today? To use the word friend, is describing you mildly, when deep down inside, you know I am wildly, mad about you, to the tenth degree, you gave my life meaning, when you choose to be with me. Yes, I am proud to call myself a man, but when it comes to you, I'm like putty in your hand. Mold me, fold me, turn me inside out, I'm rapped around your finger, beyond a shadow of doubt. When you first got a hold of what's here to work with, I was rough around the edges; there were lots of things amiss. But through dedication and commitment without cease, you turn me from a want me not, into a master piece.

#15
"CAN'T TAKE CREDIT"

*Call me what you like, I can't take credit for
how God made me. I guess it was his will, to
have the heart He gave me. I didn't
make myself, can't take credit for that,
wasn't born with wealth, my explanation for
lack. I never developed the hunger, most
people have for money, is it any wonder, some
may find it funny, the way I view, revenue,
can't miss what you never knew. So having
no flow, you know, it may make me sad,
or sometimes even mad, but it doesn't make
me bad and I'm glad.*

#16

"YOUR SUCCULANT SELF"

Dip and dab, slip and slide, glide,
deep inside. So moist and wet, and yet, my
pet, how freaky you can get. Down and
dirty, frisky and flirty, but only, with me.
How happy, I am to be, the man you chose to
see, romantically. My sweet lady, how
luscious you are, by far, the most appealing,
and sensual I've ever known, when I'm gone,
I can't wait to come home, so we can be
alone. With your succulent self, wearing a
sexy teddy, and nothing else, always ready to
please me, as need be.

#17
"SO CRAZY"

Strike a spark, light the dark, walk in the park, swim with a shark. I don't care what we do, as long as I can do it with you. I hope you can see, how crazy, I am, about the way, you sway. You are by far, my shining star. Just want you to know, I don't want you to go. Bordering on astronomical, and can at times, be quite comical. Oh so tantalizing, always mesmerizing, amazingly hypnotic, full of wisdom and logic. I could go on and on, talking about the ways, you rock my world, but it suffices to say, how glad I am, to call you my girl.

#18
"NO, TWO, WAYS"

Most people, have come to the conclusion, being perfect, is an illusion. Personally, I disagree. You can, obtain this objective, if you, keep the right perspective. Be selective, pick and choose, refuse, to use and abuse, don't be confused. There is right and wrong, no two ways about it. Be aware, of what is fair, never live without it. Life should be a dream; we could live serene, if we would learn, not to be so extreme.
Many thirst, to do their worst, destruction and mayhem, they think of first. Naturally, is the way to be, it is the only way, to be truly free.

#19
"LOVE KNOWS NO BOUNDS"

What do you say, to someone that's your everything, when words, are just not enough? Life has dealt, you a devastating blow, but there are some things, and you just have to let them know. Like, you are my first, and my last, my beginning, and my end. My start, and my finish, these things, no amount of time, can diminish. My sun, my moon, my air, and my water, without you in it, my life has no order. The food I eat, the heart beat in my chest, until I can hold you again, my spirit can find no rest. All these statements, may sound, really profound, but when it comes to you, my love, knows no bounds. This is not exaggeration, or, an over active imagination, you are, my inspiration. I sincerely mean, every word, you've heard. My only wish is that I, could better articulate, in order, to more accurately communicate, the appeal, for you I feel. So let it be known, after all is said and done, that when it comes, to my one and only true love, you are the one.

#20

"IN THE FLESH"

There are many things to celebrate in our universe, what we are blessed to celebrate, is not even our first. Existence has blessed us, to do this a second time around, out of everything ever made, you are the best thing I've found. This is something that mere words, cannot best express, it has to be demonstrated, in the flesh.

#21
"OVER THE HUMP"

At such a time as this, when things are really amiss, we need to know, where to turn, when for our love one, we do yearn. Yes, we know, they are in a better place, still, we, wish, to see their face. We love them, miss them, want them here, this love one who's gone, we hold so dear. Where is our comfort, at this trying time, what do we hold on to, for our peace of mind? How about the thought, that they are in paradise, now tell me, aren't thinking a thought like that, really very nice? They have gone to meet their maker; something we all hope to do, fortunately for them, their dream has come true. So will ours one day, as we live by and by and we will see them once again, so there's no need to cry. This life is but a layover, for all of us you see, while we await for the day, when God, sets our spirits free. So don't be heavy hearted, or down in the dump, for our love one you see, has gone over the hump.

#22
"YES"

Hello baby, this is just to let you know, yes, you drive me crazy. Yes, I have you on my mind, not just once in a while, but all of the time. Yes, how the thought of you makes me smile, the things you do, makes it all worthwhile. Yes, to me you are the best. I have no need, to look at the rest. Yes, I have made my mind up, the deal, is sealed. Yes, I am in it for the duration, there is, no limitation, to what I will do, for you. Yes, I am as happy, as can be. Yes, I do, love you. Yes, my quest, for that special someone, is done. By the way, did I say yes?

#23
"OPENING LINE"

I don't know you, and you don't know me, but together, the both of us can become we. That all depends, on how you feel, and whether or not, you are attracted, to my sex appeal. I have heard, a little about you, here and there, I'm hoping to learn, a whole lot more, if you are willing to share. Your inner-most thoughts, deepest, darkest secrets, and fantasies you have, that you can let me in on, with no regrets. I have a few of my own, when I think of you, I can't wait to come home, and make a few, come true. There will be plenty of time for that, as I get to now you better, you can start by sending me a pic-

ture, when you write your first letter. I antic-
ipate the arrival of some sweet spoken word,
let's see if you can think of something, I have
never heard. In the meantime, I will dream of
the day, when you send something my way, to
say, I am here to stay. Until then, consider
me, a special friend.

#24
"MAN"

Dr. Seuss wrote stories in rhyme, all the
time. This was very clever; however,
they were a fictitious creation, from his
imagination. I will write about life.
Father, mother, sister, brother,
husband, and wife. Then you have children, if you are of mind, you know we
have to perpetuate, the continuation of
mankind. The subjects and topics will

not stay the same, so make sure you pay attention, to notice the change. I, at the time of this writing, am forty-five years old, and have decided it is time, for some things, to be told. Like how the world has turned, into such a disgrace, I am ashamed, to call myself, a part of the human race. My, how we have made, such a mess of things, I declare, it's a crying shame. Crime and corruption, from the capital, to the hood, everywhere you look, people are up to no good. All in the name, of getting ahead, the planet would be better off, if we were all dead. Because, once our feet, hit the floor, all we want, is more, more, more. Nothing is ever enough for us, and everywhere we go, always in a rush. Faster, higher, farther, why bother? Just to reach, our doom, so soon. Now I don't mean to sound so morbid, but you have to admit, people can be, so sordid. Just look at the things, we have done for whatever, when we are capable of doing, so much better. It breaks my heart, the way different races, are always fussing and fighting, over different places. Some of us actually, consider this exciting. But you know, what the really bad part is, when there is no one else to find, we will even turn on our own kind. Now tell me, if that's not sick and twisted, how fast our rage, and raft has shifted. From one, to another, we will even kill, our own brother. It is low down dirty and insane, man can be, so deranged, that he will deface the earth, all in the name of profit, and increasing his net worth. The jails are running over, with people of all types, putting it on TV, making it the hype. And people are really interested, in what goes on behind bars, like it was discovering, the existence of life on mars. And yes, the exploration of space is vitally important to us, to find out, if there, is another home, out there, somewhere, is a must. Because, here, we are polluting the air, contaminating the water, running through the resources of this one, like mad men, even the soil itself, we have done damage in. for what, our survival, the planet is not our rival. But we are acting, as though it has a vendetta, to get back at us, for what we have taken, but we are mistaken. It was designed to keep giving, as long as we keep living. Man seems to have yet to learn, that there has to be balance in nature, as long as he, keep insisting, on being one sided, the longer we, the people of the world, will be divided. There is more, than enough, stuff in the world, to go around, but a few, wanted to keep most of it, to themselves, making the rest of us

frown. Through greed, selfishness, and fear, not wanting to let,
anyone else near, the bounty, the world has to offer readily, but don't, get ahead of me. This use to be, the land of the free, but now, you can't even do, what you want behind closed doors, without people kicking them in, yelling, pointing a gun, and daring you to run. They are wearing badges, threatening to fire, nothing but henchmen, for hire. Throwing you down, on the ground, knee on your head, fight back, and you may be dead. To serve and protect, your rights, they reject, willfully neglect, to mirandize, failing to apprise, you of the facts, being lacks, in their duty, even apprehending you, with a cutie, wearing her tight jeans, showing her booty. What an embarrassment, to see, this lady officer, assailing me.

#25
"HOPE"

Want not, as it is written, but we all
have desire, food we require. We need a
place to live, nice clothes to
wear, someone home, when we get
there. Friends to spend time with, giving
a love one, some kind of gift. Getting a
present for yourself, a pot of gold would
bring you wealth. A dream comes true,
for me and you. A fantasy, you would
like to be. Hope, in all shapes and
sizes, life is full, of many surprises. Some
good, some bad, some make you happy,
some make you sad. Come what may,
hope is never giving up, no matter what.

#26
"CLOSER TO YOU"

We have been, together for some time, being away from you, is all that's on my mind. I am going crazy, wishing I was by your side, my feeling for you, I can no longer hide. You mean so much to me, I can't find the words to say, I dream about you constantly, all night, and every day. I can't wait, until we are walking hand in hand, so I can tell, you how glad I am, to be your man. I know there are things, we need to work out, but together, we can in love, of this I have no doubt. I am thinking of you, yesterday, today, and ever more, so know in your heart, that you are the one I adore.

#27
"KNOWING YOU CARE"

What a relief it is, to know you are on my side, helping me, looking out, doing what you can, even though I may not ask, because of my pride. I am very grateful, for the things you do for me, I would like to show my gratitude, when I finally become free. At the moment, my hands are tied, in a manner of speaking, and I can't tell you how, knowing you are there, helps keep me from weeping. Some may say, a real man should never cry, but it's not about shedding tears, but a soulful, heartfelt sigh. This is my way of saying, thank you very much, for listening, not dissing, just blessing me and such.

#28
"REAL LIVE PRINCESS"

How long has it been, since someone said
my friend, you are such a fox, you knock
me out of my socks. There are billions of
women on the planet; you are one with
looks that should be carved in granite. I
consider myself lucky, you are far from
being, an ugly ducky. A real live
princess, before my eyes,
one who loves me, to my pleasant
surprise. I say out loud, I am proud, to
be among the few, who can say, they can
lay, a claim to you.

#29

"NO GREATER LOVE"

Destiny works in mysterious ways, how is it treating you these days? Do you ever think of when we first met, I still have yet, to have regret? Even though we are apart, I carry you always, in my heart. These are words, just to say, I am missing you, every day. So hang in there, hold on tight, in due time, everything will be alright. I will never forget, what you gave of your life, there's no greater love, than selfless sacrifice. I thank you so much, for being there for me you have proven yourself, to the tenth degree. No matter how long I live, I will always remember, how you were willing to give, total surrender, of your freedom, and your good name, if I ever have the chance, I will do the same.

#30
"DEVINE INTERVENTION"

I'm going to make this short but sweet, to let you know, I'm glad we had the chance to meet. Is it just my imagination, that a true vision of God's creation, could capture my attention, and please let me mention, that being held captive by you would be an overdue, dream come true. To be your prisoner of love could only be, divine intervention, sent from above.

#31
"LET IT BE KNOWN"

You do understand, that I think about you all the time... right, from when the sun comes up in the morning, until the stars shine at night. The thing I regret the most, is having you out of my sight. I lay here and imagine, us having fun, one on one, enjoying each other's pleasure, oh how I treasure, the time we share, knowing you care, always there. I cherish the gift, I have been blessed with. So let it be known, if I sat on a thrown you would be, sitting beside me

#32

"THE FUN TO COME"

Just a little something to say, I figured I would take the time today, to send a few thoughts your way. I hope this finds you feeling well, without seeing you, I can-not tell. I am trying to put, a smile on your face, hoping to lift your spirits, in this dismal place. A day you don't laugh

is one you waste. So have a ha ha, he, he,
giggle on me in case you're sad, you can
cheerfully, think about the fun to come,
when we both are free.

#33
"THE MAGIC OF WORDS"

Writing poetry has to do with sensory,
It's not all about, making since, you
see? The magic of words, saying things
you've never heard. Playing a game,
not saying the same,
as others have before, yet said
evermore. Over and over, by someone
new, thoughts you once had, inside of
you. Now out in the open, for the world
to see, you think, just think, these words
were once, inside of me.

#34
"OBSESSION"

What is it with man, why does he do everything he can, destroying the earth, trying to increase his net worth. There is nothing wrong with wanting to get ahead, but does it have to come at the cost, of other creatures being unnecessarily dead. Why can't we, live in harmony, is it necessary, for us, to make a mess, of the rest, of the planet, instead of doing our best, to caress, what we take for granted. No, it's not all, but this world is so small, it is not going to last forever, so we, need to care for it better. This should be our obsession; we need to make a correction.

#35
"YOU NEED TO KNOW"

The love I have inside of me, you set my feelings free, the man I want to be. You need to know who, I have to show you, the kind of man I, will not just stand by, and let you go, you need to know. You I adore, each passing day, I love you more. I know you might say, these words are OK, but actions speak louder, they have the power. That's what matters most, from the east to the west coast. As man, has concurred land, so have you, captured me too. And you need to know, I will never, ever, let you go.

#36
"CARNAL CONSTRUCTION"

We have reached, that unattainable plateau, arrived at a destination, sought by so many, found by so few, maintained by even less. We started with a foundation, grounded in commitment. We progressed to framing, with dedication and determination. We proceeded with siding, of tolerance and patients. We laid flooring, with understanding. We walled rooms of forgiveness, windows of motivation, and doors of inspiration. We topped it all above, with a roof of love. Then we furnished it with passion, tenderness, intimacy and admiration.

#37
"TIME AND SPACE"

Let's take this to the next level, a higher plain. We are going to traverse the cosmos, light years to attain, in a matter of minutes, the expanse of time and space, we will be in it. The wonders of the universe, will unfold before us, like an open book all it will take, is for us to look. Secrets, revealed to us, just for the asking, as if it were a must.
The darkness of its depths will be a shining beacon of light,
in the dense blackness of endless night. This is what the acknowledgment, of our love for each other will do. No more mystery, we will go down in history.

#38
"COULDN'T BE BETTER"

It's another day we can thank God, we live to see. I thank God that, you are still with me. I don't know, what I would do, if I had, to live without you.
I guess I would go crazy,
have I told you lately,
how you daze me.
Stunning is an accurate acronym, the way the Master built you, is just a knack for Him. The way He put you together, He couldn't have done better. You are perfect, the way He made you, and you couldn't make me happier, even if I paid you.

#39
"LAST BUT NOT LEAST"

Holidays come but once a year, it starts
when the arrival, of a new one is here.
Then we celebrate, the birth of a man
named Martin Luther King, how he
lived his life, a wonderful thing, finally
we end, celebrating the birth, of another
King. But what amazes me, is not his
birth you see, because it was his death,
which set our spirits free. Of His life, He
freely gave, to save all of us, from death
hell and the grave. But first, He was
given birth, saying whomever shall drink
of the living water, shall never thirst. So
it is at this time, that we celebrate, the
life that made, this man great.

#40
"FEELINGS WILL NEVER CHANGE"

To my girl, you know you are my world. Cut a man some slack. What's up with that? You are supposed to tell a man, what he wants to hear, like how you want to hold him near, and whisper sweet nothings in his ear. What's with this negativity, acting as though, you want to break up with me. You need to come around, don't kick a man, when he's down. When I was home, wasn't I good to you? So tell me baby, what are you going to do? I'm trying to put, these words in a way, to have the greatest effect, on what I have to say. My feelings for you, will never change, yesterday, today, tomorrow, they will still be the same. You are sweet, you are sexy, you are every man's dream, aren't you glad you met me? What I say are things I mean, I know I'm not there, to tell you these

things, in the flesh, but with pen and paper, I
will do my best, to remind you over and over,
of all these things, to convince you as best I
can, not to let your feelings change.

#41
"MY CARE GIVER"

To my attending nurse, without you, my
stay here, would be a lot worse. Thank
you so much, for coming around, if it
wasn't for getting my pills, I would
really be down. Being trapped in here is
bad enough, and being sick, to
boot, makes it really rough. So bless your
heart, you and your little cart, I don't
care, what others may say, but I am
glad, to see you every day. And I
know, I can be difficult on occasion, but

a few kind words, works as well,
as medication.

#42
"A CHANGED MAN"

There was a movie called "Lady Sings the Blues", well I know how it feels, to be in her shoes. Because, being away from you, is killing me, like a sergeant in boot camp, drilling me. How can I keep, doing the things I do, knowing I could possibly, be taken away from you? My actions, contradict themselves, when all the time, I convict myself. Not having you, by my side, in a place like this, I reside. While you are out there, roaming free, when all the while, you should be with me. Wining, dining, and taking you places, but being apart, these things leave know traces. But things will be

*different, from here on out, of this fact,
please have known doubt. From now on,
I am a changed man, and we will soon
be walking the aisle, hand in hand.*

#43
"BEYOND IMAGINATION"

*Hello sweetheart, this is just a little
something, nothing fancy or
extravagant, merely a few
words, written to no certain extent, to
let you know, how I feel about you, but
I'm sure after all this time, this is
nothing new. Oh how you still blow my
mind, to me, you are one of a kind. There
is a song that says, "one in a
million", but it would be more accurate,
to call you, one in a billion. This is not
exaggeration; you have fulfilled dreams
of mine, beyond my wildest*

imagination. So, I just want to let you know, that I never want to let you go. I don't care, if I have to buy you a Packard, or like Clark Kent, in "Superman", make the world spin backward. In other words, there is no limit, to what I will do, to prove to you, my love is true. In the movie "Titanic", the woman called herself a "dish", well, like the Jeannie in a lamp, I say, go ahead, make a wish. And watch me astound you, beyond your wildest dreams, amaze you with feats, you have never seen. You won't believe, the things you see as I show you, the love I have in me.

#44
"BREAKING THE ICE"

The thoughts I have of you, may be construed as lewd, but my intentions, are to entrance and romance. I want to be a pleasant surprise, mesmerize, almost hypnotize too, as you have done, me to you. Can you see the affect you have had on me? Please don't reject, my advances, until you at least, give a man a few chances, to prove himself, and show that he is in to you, and no one else. Not meaning to sound, like I'm begging, but please, don't dismiss a man, until you at least, see my plan, to make your toes tingle, and make your heart jingle.

#45
"INSPIRATION"

Life, does not come, with an instruction
book, we should look, living each day, as
if it were our first, or our last. The past,
has, influence on our future. But all we
ever have is the present. We have, to
make the best of it. It will not
always, turn out as we would like, but
once in a while, something happens, to
make us smile. Things, unexpected, out
of the blue, so don't reject it, have a new,
perspective. A fresh outlook, a renewed
vigor, you hadn't had before, pursue
with rigor. Carry on; more and more
strive to attain height's you've never
reached before.

#46
"SPIRITUALITY"

According to Christian scripture, Jesus Christ, gave his life, as a sacrifice, that in itself, should make you be nice. Love, share, dare, to care, for your father, mother, sister, brother, husband and wife, you shouldn't need to think twice. Friend or foe, stranger you meet, walking the street. By faith, through grace, do not be, a waste of space. Leave a trace, of your days, displayed, for all to see, who you came to be, internally, for all eternity. Eternally unique, diligently discrete, let no man, know your hand, for as long as you can, withstand, the grand plan, for the land.

#47
"SOMEONE SPECIAL"

Someone special, a special
someone, being with them, is like a
lottery you've won. Someone special, a
special someone, a person with whom,
you have lots of fun. Someone special, a
special someone, from the stars at night,
to the rising sun. Someone special, a
special someone, giving thanks every
time, a new day has begun. Someone special, a special someone, flirtations from
others, you automatically shun. Someone
special, a special someone, this is only
the beginning, there is more to
come. Someone special, a special
someone, there is a song about, "love on
the run". Someone special, a special
someone, if it meant saving you, I would
move a ton. Someone special, a special

someone, it would really be great,
if you had my son.

#48
"MY FELLOW MAN"

For my fellow man, we should do whatever
we can, but we don't, or we won't. I don't
know why, it brings tears to my eye. Don't
we hear our fellow man's cries? I need, May I
have, would you please, is how they
plead. But their words go unheard, as if
speaking in silence, a whisper in the wind,
come again. We say, maybe, one day, I may,
do what I can, for my fellow man.

#49
"JUST BECAUSE"

For the sake of doing, I cater to
you, there is nothing in the world, that I
won't do. Just the mere thought, of you
having to go without, makes me shiver,
and quiver, to make your desires, come
about. It's just because, I care for
you, and I want you to know, my love is
true. I can't believe, the way you make
me feel, that's why I know,
your love is real.
The way you treat me, is beyond
belief, and I will never do anything, to
cause you grief.

#50
"ALL OR NOTHING"

Happily ever after, as it happens in fairy
tales is desired by some men,
but most females. Prince charming,
a knight in shining armor,
looking for a man, she knows, will never
harm her. Protect her, all of the time,
completely, blows her mind, romance her
when at home, take her out to wine and
dine. Make her his wife; be with her for
life, doing special things, making her
feel nice. She doesn't want
half-hearted, hesitation just won't do,
you must finish what you started, show
her your love is true. All or nothing is
what she looks for, even when she finds
it, she may still, look for more.

#51
"HONEST TO GOODNESS"

Just for you, I want you to know it,
my love is true, and this is to show it.
Beyond rhyme or reason, any time,
across space, no matter the season,
no one can replace, the love for you,
I have inside, this is nothing new,
and I say it with pride. From now,
until, the end of time, I promise, I will,
try to make you mine. In everything I
do, in every word I say, I will show
you, I am here to stay. So don't be
skeptical, or in disbelief, I hope you find
me acceptable, and not cause me grief.
Put me at ease, so I can relax, let me
appease, you to the max. Time will tell,
as it passes by, you will know well,
I am no lie.

#52
"TWO-WAY STREET"

Mutual attraction and desire, not a
companion for hire. Two consenting adults,
no strings attached, the kind of involvement,
a free spirit attracts. Not pinned down, by a
ball and chain, pouring emotions into
something, hoping for something to gain. Only
living for the moment, trying to have a good
time, never being phony,
or messing with your mind.

#53
"UPS AND DOWNS"

There are no guarantees in life, so before
you make a decision, you better think
twice. You never know, what lies ahead,
make the wrong turn, you could wind up

dead. Be careful, use caution in everything you do, the first time you do it, everything is new. You may succeed, you may fail, but the bottom line, is to live to tell the tale.

#54

"BITTER WITH THE SWEET"

Good or bad, it could be the worst day, you've ever had. You wonder why, you even got out of bed; you think to yourself, I'd rather be dead. You find it amazing, how awful things are, and it puts you in the mind, of a bug in a jar. Once upon a time, as free as a bird, now look at yourself, feeling lower than a turd. But for most people, that is how life is, here today, gone tomorrow, so don't let your present, be filled with sorrow.

#55
"SINK OR SWIM"

Jump in, the deep end, stroke for all you're worth, this is, how it has been, from the moment of our birth. You have to crawl before you walk, cry before you talk. Answer the call of nature, when it comes, in time, we should all, stop sucking on our thumbs. Some of us may, get carried away, but if you want to break a habit, you keep at it, like the energizer rabbit.

#56
"RAIN OR SHINE"

Sometimes, the weather is dreary, like it is today, sometimes things make you leery, and this too, is OK. The trials of life can be unnerving, but this should suffice, to make you deserving, of the things you have, or the things you get, and just maybe, you haven't seen anything yet. If you live, long enough, you will go through some things, but it doesn't take a lifetime, for you to earn your wings. Children g to heaven, all the time, and this is the end, of my heavenly rhyme.

#57
"A BRUSH WITH DEATH"

You never know, how close you are, to a visit, from the Grim Reaper. It's only by faith, through grace, that the Supreme Being, let's your life line run deeper. To stay on earth, for an extended time, so in all your endeavors, keep this in mind. Tomorrow will not, always arrive; no one gets out, of this life alive. So take each day, as if it were your

last, for the time will come, for you too
to pass.

#58
"NARROW ESCAPE"

Talk about a close call, you've come to
the edge, and about to fall.
Then somehow, miraculously, you are
given a way, to get out scout free. You
had no idea, when you first began, what
would deliver you, to the Promised
Land. Now here you are, to pleasant
surprise, reality unfolding, right before
your eyes. You take a deep
breath, breathe a sigh of relief, you have
gotten out of, a whole lot of grief. It is
refreshing, to make a narrow escape,
when you come out ahead, you must
admit, it is really great.

#59
"SILENCE IS BLISS"

Sometimes you want peace and quiet, so desperate at times, you are willing to buy it. No matter where you are, near or far, you can't get away from noise, like a room full of kids, playing with toys. Ruckus and racket, everywhere you turn, oh how you yearn, for somewhere to hide, a solitary place, for you to reside. Madness and mayhem, all over the place, you wish it would vanish, without a trace. Deep down you believe, silence is bliss, and, at times, above all else, this is what you miss.

60
"ACCIDENTS HAPPEN"

Unexpected, out of the blue, the next
thing you know, someone has, blindsided
you. Caught off guard, blown away,
what once was blissful, is now a tragic
day. An unintended mishap, you took
the wrong turn, it can happen in sec-
onds, and soon you will learn, what
comes to pass, is an inevitable event,
don't dwell on what was, because it was
meant. It's not for us to wonder
why, things will happen, by and
by. Accidents occur, that's a fact of
life, and the important thing is,
not to let it happen twice.

#61
"RAT RACE"

The hustle and bustle, of day to day activity,
has always seemed, amazing to me. This perfectly
synchronized, unscripted choreography
has evolved throughout time, to perfect
simplicity. It is so predictable at times, it has
become subconscious, even routine, and if you've
done the same thing for years, you know what I
mean. We almost seem programmed, the way we go
about things, as if being controlled by
someone, pulling on our strings. Caught in this rat
race, running through mazes, and the events in our
life, happen in stages. We are conceived, we are
born, after high school, from our parents, we are
torn. To go out in the world, and make our
way, this is a natural course of action, some may
say. But does it have, to go like this, getting out of
your comfort zone, taking such risk. I know, it's
because, no one's the same, finding your own
way, is the name of the game.

#62
"CUT DEEP"

Taking everything to heart, getting bent out of shape, letting your feathers get ruffled, huffing and puffing, like an ape. It's not that serious, when someone pulls your leg, getting your panties in a bunch, because of something someone said. It's not always meant, to get under your skin, let it roll like water, off of a ducks back, and then, come back at them, with a jest of your own, show them that, it means nothing, and they will leave you alone. Like an untrained dog, snapping at your leg, he will leave you in peace, if you hit him, in his head.

#63
"AT FIRST GLANCE"

For some, emotions run deep, and others,
you will never see them weep. Their
hearts are like stone, it would be
better, to leave them alone.
Unfeeling, unyielding, like a glacier of
solid ice, nothing appealing. A frozen
tundra, never to melt, a compassionate
moment, they have never felt.
No remorse, never to waiver, like food
you eat, that has no flavor. It would
do, to sustain yourself, but you would
much rather, have something else. You
want it to make, your taste-buds dance,
picked out of a buffet, at first glance.
Not so, with some you know, just goes
to show, it is best, to let them go.

#64
"FLAWLESS"

There is something, about natural perfection, that unseen force, behind random selection. All things seem, to fall in place, flaws and fallacies, leave no trace, of the way they intrude, on the human race, allowing some to live, without disgrace. It's quite a feat, this plateau to meet, showing no fault, almost a, clairvoyant result, It's not about being, full of yourself, it's just to set an example, for someone else.

#65
"JUST A FRIEND"

What is it going to take, to keep you from making a mistake? You are still looking around, when there are few like me, to be found. Acting like, I am a dime a dozen, when you already, found your husband. Your options you are weighing, relentlessly playing, the field, not ready to be for real. I don't know, why this is, when you say you want, to have my kids. When I speak, I talk with zeal, but you don't seem, to know the deal. How hard could this be, when I show, all of me? Ever stop to wonder, before we go asunder, what could be, between you and me? You only see, what's before your eyes, but by faith, through grace, you could get a surprise. Feats beyond your wildest dream, but you, have no clue, what I mean. Astonishment, our life would garnish with. A precious gift to internally uplift. I've been telling you this for years, but my words, fall on deaf ears. And since it hasn't sunken in, you just want, to be my friend. Then what's a man supposed to do, except look to find him, someone new? Forgave you time and time again, overlooking, and extracurricular men. These are the facts, what more can you ask? Entice, re-splice, giving more than twice. It amazes me, to see, you be, completely, clueless, when we could do this. Yet, it doesn't sink in, you just want, to be my friend. The more I show, the less you know, blind, to the ways of man-kind. Using you, abusing you, the things they do, confusing you. Only filling your life with dread, keeping you from getting ahead. Let me make a correction, this is no deception, no

need, to mislead, I'm the
exception. Unlike those, you are
accustoming to, I'm trying to put, my
trust in you. But you refuse, to
comprehend, you just want,
to be my friend.

#66
"NO BLOOD TIES"

For no special reason, not due to, any
given season. Just for the hell of
it, hoping you think well of it. Out of
the kindness of my heart, not for us
being apart. Only to say, I'm thinking of
you today. So take this,
as it comes, costing no, elaborate sums.
It's only just a dime a dozen, no more
than if you were my cousin. Even

without, having blood ties, this should come, as no surprise. I think of you, as my brother, by another mother.

#67
"PACKAGE DEAL"

Don't try to use me, to get your thrill, when none of my desires, you care to fulfill. One hand washes the other, the door swings both ways, if we are, to be together, and this is how it stays. Scratch my back, I'll scratch yours; stop leaving me hanging, with all of the chores. I cater to you, make you feel good, there are things I want too, I wish that you would. Bring a smile to my face; put some joy in my heart, a void to replace, this is a start. I am willing; to go that extra mile, do whatever it takes, to make you smile. Making you happy, is what I live for, if I haven't done enough, I will do more. Oh my, you and I, for goodness sake, what a team we would make. As I live and breathe, you wouldn't believe, how happy we are, like a shining star. I want that twinkle, in your eye, to thank my lucky stars, and wonder why, when you looked my way, you didn't pass me by. People look, much of their lives, trying to fill, a void inside. They are hoping, for someone, to take up space that needs undone. We search and seek, every day of the week, wine and dine, wishing to find, a love, exceptional, never be, questionable. Seek and you shall find, is the teaching of, all mankind. This is what, we are told, it will be proven, as we grow old. Time and again, we desire a friend, to turn into, someone new, whose love, will be true. Up and down, makes us frown, an emotional bug, going around. We hang in there, through all despair, waiting to find, someone to care. I was glad, I found you, to look no more, for someone new. You and I became we, what comes to pass, was meant to be. Having you, by my side, filled me up, with lots of pride. I took solace, in our love; felt it sent, from above. Divine intervention, I rather see, whenever you are with me. We, could have, a lot to be thankful for in time to come, we would thank for more. I can, put your mind at ease, help your heart relax, and show, I want to please, you, to the max. What we, should have together, please know, I want forever.

#68
"A DELIMA FOR ME"

Sitting in a cell, wasting time, all kinds of thoughts, going through my mind. From what's going on with my girl, to what's happening in the world. This is not the place to be; at least it's not, the place for me. You can come and stay, if you like, but I don't care to spend the night. I can't see how, some come and go, back to back, I tell you now, and I'm not with that. Many of you might say it's no big deal, but you are the ones, not keeping it real. This is a matter; you take to heart, when you, your friends and love ones, are miles apart. In some cases, it could mean life or death. But that's seldom a problem, for those with wealth.

#69

"LIFE AND DEATH"

This is reality, even if it isn't, since to
me, this is how, it's meant to be. You
can't have one, without the other, no
need to try, they come together. Flooded
with joy, crushed with sadness,
for feeble minds, this could be madness.
Cruelty, and atrocities, emphasize, with
apostrophes. Life and death, comes and
goes, where we end up, no one knows.
Numerous speculations, for men to
consider, but in the end, we all, wreak
and whither.

#70
"SOLITARY"

Just another form, of the norm, no longer
in a dorm, but alone in a cell, it's just as
well. In shackles or chains, bondage is
just the same. Being a social
creature, taking away this life bearing
feature, this in itself, is like taking away
a man's wealth. Yes he will still be alive,
but inside, he has died. In solitary, as
implied, is not how man should reside?
In a state of being alone, when already,
far away from home.

#71
"BROTHER TO BROTHER"

My brother, just thinking of you, makes
me smile, I remember how I would
always; try to copy your style. I thought
you were so cool, suave, debonair,
nobody's fool. With me from the start,
we were never apart. If I tried to run
and fall, you were the first one, I would
call. So sorry to hear, about the bad
news, but please don't let,
it give you the blues.

#72

"A MAN'S LIFE"

On the wings of the wind, I soar
free, not restricted by the bonds of
captivity. My spirit is in motion, like a
fish in the ocean. Aloft in space, as a
bird, with effortless grace. Imagination
is a part of creation. Otherwise, it would
be our demise. Man feels a power greater
than he, led him to be. A force beyond
our control, for millenniums,
is what we've been told.

#73
"DOING SOMETHING NEW"

Why do we mourn, feel remorse, instead
of rejoice, upon someone's
passing, knowing no life,
is everlasting. Where and when, did this
tradition start, that says to have, a
heavy heart, when we lose those close to
us, like it's a given, as if it's a must.
Well I'm sorry, I'm getting out of this
mode, feeling this way, because I was
told. It's been handed down for
generations; I feel it's time for
celebrations. Celebrating the life that
was, just because, it's the right thing to
do, after all, this could be you, at any
given point in time, this is the thing, we
should keep in mind. Don't be sad, don't
feel blue, why don't we try, doing
something new. Let's go against the
grain, think outside the box, stop going

with the flow, like a river filled with rocks. How do I lose so you understand, after all, I am only a man. I don't have all the answers, to every question; I'm just trying, to make a suggestion. I feel there has to be a better way, to spend the day, recognizing the life, no longer here, saying goodbye, to the one we hold dear. I know, if it was me, I wouldn't want you unhappy, with a face full of tears, on the contrary, don't make me worry, send me off with cheers. Smiles on your face, and joy in your heart, when you give attention, to the day I depart. And, so I ask you to do this now, reach deep inside, find the strength somehow.

#74
"THE CAVIAR OF CANDY BAR"

Chocolate, nougat, peanuts, and cara-
mel, a flavor so good, it makes your taste
buds yell. A treat so sweet, it gives pure
delight, and brings a smile to your face,
with each mouth-watering bite.
If J. D. Powers, gave awards,
like they do for cars, Snickers would get
the trophy, for being, best candy bars.
When it comes to something,
for between meal snacks,
you can't go wrong with Snickers, there
is nothing it lacks. Delicious
and nutritious, the caviar of candy
bar, if you had to give it a rank, it
would be five stars. Calling it junk food,
just seems so mean, it's more like dining,
on gourmet cuisine.

#75
"STUCK TOGETHER"

Most of the time, you correctional facility guards are shown no appreciation. But that's due, mainly to our own aggravation. I know you all have a job to do, but just because we are all pissed off is no excuse for us to take our frustrations out on you. Yes, we are living in stressful days, and the moods of both of us, swings both ways, because some of you, can be cranky too, yet, at least, you're being here, pays. I don't know about your spiritual belief, but it may help you, not to cause me emotional grief, if those of you, whom I can persuade, would take the time, to go get laid. I'm just saying, for goodies sakes, let's do, whatever it takes, to make our interactions better, since we are all, stuck together. I am already disgusted,

about not being free, so I would be,
grateful, if life has made you hateful,
not to take it out on me. In return, I
will take the time, to say thanks, now
and then, if you would show, a little
compassion, for the predicament, I am
in. Lastly, although I can't give all of
you raises, I can give, some of you
praises. While I am still, unavoidably
present, I plan, to do whatever I can, to
make your job, deplorably pleasant. Now
that you have heard, please,
pass the word.

#76
"IN ALL FAIRNESS"

What can you say, about Mother's Day?
Like the James Bond movie, The World

Is Not Enough, that's how it is, between mothers, and her kids. There is nothing, they won't do or give, as long as, it is beneficial, for us to live. Safe and sound, without a care, no matter when we call, they will always be there. Making sacrifices we may never ever know of, just one of the many ways, they use to show love. Even in disappointment, when we let them down, they will still help us, all be it, with a frown. Because we have misbehaved, and made them mad, when in all fairness, they are mostly sad. Knowing that we are capable of so much better, able to do, the things we need to, to keep families together. Bottom line, mothers are so dear, a day is not sufficient, they deserve the whole year.

#77
"A WOUNDED ANIMAL"

Thinking about you sweetheart, how is my baby, can't help but to wonder, are you still my lady? Miss you so much, it's driving me out of my mind, why haven't you been to see me, in such a long time? Are you so busy, having so much fun, did you kick me to the curb, to be with someone? My heart goes all aflutter, to think of you, with another. The idea of that just blows me away, trying to imagine you, with another man today. Involuntary panic sets in, to think of the possibility that you have found another romantic friend. I can't bear the thought, as I sit here and gaze outside, I have to admit, and it has taken a toll on my pride. I'm like a wounded animal; with no help in sight, and it get even worse, when the sun sets at night. I can only hope and pray, that when I do come home, I have no need to cry. I really do, love you. Believe that, it's a fact.

#78

"MY HEART YERNS"

My mind is on you baby, can't help myself, I just hope, you haven't left me, for someone else. I don't know if I can take it, I would feel shame and disgrace, couldn't even walk the street, showing my face. The humiliation of it all would really fall, down so deep, doing, nothing but weep. Not wanting to live, there's nothing I wouldn't give, to have you again, be just my special friend. Being paranoid, imagination running wild, the last time we spoke, you said you were with child.

Asked you, who's it was, said you don't know, wondered, if that was your way of saying, it was time, for me to go? Has it been that many, that you have lost tract, couldn't you have waited, for me to come back? Oh how my heart yearns, to be with you, I dread to think, of the day, when you and I are through. God says, forgive and love above all else, how I would gladly do that, to have you, all to myself.

#79
"SELFLESS SACRIFICE"

The irreplaceable you, what a true, blessing you are, a gift from God, sent from afar. Don't know, what I would do, if you were not there for me, the way you have, accepted responsibility. I thank you, thank you, thank you, from the bottom of my heart, and that's not all, it's only the start. I exude, gratitude. To me, you are a living treasure, constantly giving, giving, giving, beyond the utmost measure. Mere words, cannot fully express, my gratefulness. With appreciation, for how you've stepped up, even while, facing your own complication. What a grand gesture, finding ultimate pleasure, the way you sacrifice, a shining example, of what it means, to be, a true, follower of Christ. To God be the glory, for putting the anointing on you, after saying that, now I am through.

#80
"FIRE AND DESIRE"

I like to take the time, once and a while, to let you know, the many ways, you make me smile. I love it, when we laugh, play, and joke around, the feelings, that you give me, are so profound. Using words, to tell you, just how special, I think you are, is like trying to catch, a shooting star. It's impossible, to verbally say, how wonderful, you make me feel, every day. How bright, my life has become, now that you are in it, the light that shines, in my heart, you are the one, who lit.

#81
"FROM HERE ON OUT"

My darling wife, it would be an understatement, the things you missed, when you were there, going about life, blindly unaware. What you have, right before your face, taking your blessing for granted, what a low down disgrace. Better late than never, to finally see the light, given a second chance, to this time do things right. Best foot forward, from here on out, not to give you reasons, to huff, and puff, and pout. I thank my Heavenly Father, I still have a chance, to woo you with affection, and entice you with romance.

#82
"A GOOD FATHER"

The backbone, of every home, from the foundation, of creation. A strong arm, to keep you from harm, the law giver, that can make you quiver. The example you follow, no need to wallow, in sorrow. Inspiration you call, whenever you fall. The calm in the storm, from the day you were born. Yes means yes, and no means

no, we take this with us, where ever we go. The strength it takes, there is no denying, when even in failure, to keep on trying. To keep all secure, and everyone safe, with the dangers of life, lurking in every place. May at any time, have to put your life on the line, and you welcome the chance, at a moment's glance. I so many ways, I recognize you, working for days, is only part of what you do. To be a good father, requires a lot, a deadbeat dad,
is one thing you're not.

#83
"WHY I LOVE YOU"

I love you because, you are real, I can't believe, the way you make me feel. Like a warm coat, on a cold winter's day, you naturally, make me feel that way. It's not exaggerated, or made to do,

instinctively expressed, is why I love
you. No pretense, not perpetrated, you
flawlessly deliver, what existence
created. An unblemished being, I can't
believe, what I'm seeing. A vision to
behold, you deploy it subconsciously, no
need to be told. This kind of persona
can't be taught, to carry yourself,
like you have no fault.

#84
"PASSING THE TIME"

Passing the time, with nothing to do,
trying to come up with, something new.
Occupy yourself, increase your wealth,
surf the internet, when there's nothing else.
You try to maintain, hoping to gain,
coming up with ideas, can scramble your
brain. But you shoot your best shot, give it all
you've got, with any luck, something will hit

the spot. Finding something to appease me,
doesn't always come easy, but with a little
effort, the unexpected, just might please me.
So here is to finding, a little joy in life, even if
sometimes, you have to think twice.
So, be nice.

#85
"IN DEEP"

Loving you is as easy as breathing,
everything about you is pleasing. I don't
know if you I can sustain without, even
the times you complain and shout. Like
an animal, I am trapped, the love that
flows in me for you, you have tapped.
I can't escape, there's no getting away,
in it for the long haul, truly here to stay.
If you think you can, get rid of me,

better think again, and soon you will
see, you my dear, I am here to win, I feel
closer to you, than a biological twin.
Ups and downs, have no effect, I deal
with them all, with no regret. So here's
to you baby, I am so proud,
to call you my lady.

#86

"THE EYE OF THE STORM"

Calm and blissful, in the midst of
turmoil, the way water simmers,
just before it boils. It doesn't seem like,
nothing will become of it, but soon, the
steam is ready to hit. It is deceptive,
how gradual it is, but open a shaken
soda and it will fizz. The power stored
inside, no longer wants to hide. The
strength, no one knows, now, all of a
sudden, there she blows. Like a glacier,

in Yellowstone Park, welling up from
somewhere, deep in the dark. Watch out,
or you will learn, get too close,
and you will burn. It doesn't seem so,
when it's calm, yet its underestimation,
can cause you harm.

#87
"A DREAM COME TRUE"

For so long, I admired you from afar,
as if looking into the night sky, at a
distant star. Now, it is, as if, you have
fallen to earth, here for the first time, to
quench my thirst, for what I crave, before I go, to my grave. Eluding me,
missing from life, the love of a good
woman, and perspective wife. Once upon
a time, I never thought, you would ever
be mine. A fantasy, couldn't imagine,

one day, you and I, became we. To think,
the thought, not for a minute, my bed, a
day, you would be in it. Still, here you
are, sleeping away, you have had,
an exhausting day. It's a dream come
true, for you to be, so close to me.
Touching, caressing, seductively dressing,
impressing, more than you know,
I never, ever, want you to go. For the
rest of my life, striving, to make, you, my
cherished wife. Eternally, endeavor to
be, completely, oblivious, to the
distraction, and interactions, dividing
us. Staying together, under cover,
my ultimate goal, is to be your
fantasy lover.

#88
"TOP OF THE WORLD"

From terraform to orbit, exceptionally euphoric. Unforeseen, being serene. You give and you get, a once in a lifetime bet. What had been out of sight, now blinds you, the way the sun, shines its light. You can't look it in the eye, as it illuminates the sky. So bright in its intensity, taking you by surprise, makes the noon despise, the glory of its formation, a wonder to behold, the way it evolved with in creation. Starting out illusively, now in a realm of its' own exclusively. On top of the world, as around it, our planet continues to hurl.

#89
"TRAIN OF THOUGHT"

Thinking of this and that, focusing on, matters of fact. Contemplating, calculating, meditating, trying to achieve, and ascertain, what's invigorating. Clearing your mind, leaving the insignificant, far behind. What is pertinent, relevant, striving for the extravagant. Reaching for the stars, like a NASA voyage to Mars. Hitting a target, so far away, going above and beyond, every day. Dreams start in your imagination, endeavors needing, no exaggeration. Believed, and not seen, that's what the definitions of faith mean. Knowing, then showing, when others deny, having a goal beyond the sky. Finding no fault, in your own, train of thought.

#90
"TO THINE OWN SELF BE TRUE"

*Time is the only thing priceless. Compared to the
cost of any material possession, it is worth twice
this. With this in mind, in order to be of benefit to
mankind, doing everything for the following
reasons, would make me sublime. Self preservation.
Self motivation. Self defense. Self confidence. Self
reliance. Self assurance. Self fulfillment.
Self employment. Self improvement.
Self enjoyment. Self awareness. I declare Tess. Self
approval, and if necessary removal, from a negative
situation, and in small doses. even self
gradification. Self discipline, Self reflection. Self
realization. Self perception. Self acceptance,
Self esteem at times to be serene. Self control can
take a toll. Above all else, know yourself and your
net wealth. Please don't neglect, self respect.
Remember, you are what you eat,
as you sow, so shall you reap.
In order to rise, you must first go to sleep.
In so doing, you can be of benefit,
to everyone you meet.*

#91
"NO REGRET"

Loving you, is as easy as breathing, everything about you, is pleasing. There is nothing, I can complain about, you need not have, any doubt. My heart is in a trap, there is no getting away. In it for the long haul, truly here to stay. If you think you can, get rid of me, you better think again, because you see, my love for you, comes from within, I feel closer to you, than a biological twin. Up's and down's, have no effect, I deal with them all, with no regret. So here's to you, my sweet, my loving baby, I am so proud, to call you my lady.

#92
"NO MATTER WHAT"

With Valentine's Day, so nearby, I send you a gift, made in the sky. It's a heart shaped box, on a clear winter's night, with each little star, a sweet candy delight. If you made a wish, I'd make it come true, if you wished for a star, I'd give you that too. The gleam in your eyes, the glow on your face, has me mesmerized, as we stare into space. I thank my lucky stars, for the day I found you, I would explore Mars, to prove my love true. How do always love thee, till my dying days. I could never count the things, I have to thank you for, no more than I could count, the grains of sand upon the shore. I could never tell you, how much you mean to me, no more than I could tell you, how many fish are in the sea. Tell me what you want, is all I suggest, to give your heart's desire, I would go on a quest. No matter what, I will never fail, if it's what you wish, I would find the Holy Grail. You are my sunshine, my full moon at night, in my darkest hour, you can make it bright. No matter what my problem, what trouble comes my way, with you I know I'll solve them, and have a better day.

#93
"SO SWEET"

There are many sweet things in the world,
but none can compare to the flavor of my girl.
Honey comb, candy cane, many things I
cannot name. Nothing can come close to the
taste of you, I don't want anything to take
the place of you. I yearn to suck and lick,
every trace of you, from the toes on your feet,
up to the face of you. I will not miss a spot,
waste a drop, devour you over and over,
non-stop, you are my source of sustenance,
and I need a lot. So you are in for the time of
your life, like a giant Anaconda, I will eat
you twice, and the second time around, will
be equally as nice. There is no one on earth,
I would rather be my wife.

#94
"I JUST KNOW"

To my unknown future wife, the sound of that, is very nice. I can't wait until the day we meet, I just know, you will be, oh, so, sweet. I look forward to seeing your beautiful eyes, just think, everything about you, will be a surprise. The way you walk, the way you talk, my imagination runs wild, trying to picture your smile. Your hair, is it long, is it short, does it curl or hang straight, no matter how it is, I just know, it looks great. As for me, at the moment, I have been out of it for a while, I look rough and tumble, rugged of style. It has been rough, for about a year, but I can look really good, when I get it in gear. I think, I am a really nice guy, you will see, I just know, you will think so, when you get to know me.

#95

"THE FIRST TIME"

The first time, I laid eyes on you, made me weak on my feet. The first time, I heard you speak, I had to take a seat. The first time, you asked for something, you request became my order. The first time, I smelled your aroma, my mouth began to water. The first time, you smiled at me, the world became a brighter place. The first time, I made you laugh, I could see heaven, in your face. The first time, you touched my hand, I knew, I would be your man. The first time, I hold you in my arms, will set off all the car alarms. The first time, I make love to you, I will know, you love me too.

#96
"NO MISTAKEN"

I want to take the time, to let you to know,
what you mean to me, and that I love you so.
I know, others may throw, these words
around, just for show. But I don't believe in
faking, or perpetrating, these comments I
make, let there be, no mistaken. What I say,
is honest and sincere, please understand, I
hold you dear. If feelings had weight, they
would weigh a ton, my heart, you have won.
Yes, this is heavy, for me, seriously, happy,
that, you and I, became we. My one and only,
lady. I will let, you reflect, on this for a
while, I hope, it makes you smile,
as a woman, who is with child. Wow, how, I
like your style.

#97

"I SALUTE YOU"

Hey mom, has it been long, since I wrote you a sonnet, do you get, it? Smiley face :-), just a taste, of my gratefulness, for your grace fullness, please forgive, my wastefulness. I know, I took for granted, at times, things I've had, that were mines, For a while, they brought a smile, to my lips so easy, the things I would get and do, just to please me. Not thinking about how, in a heartbeat, my sustenance could be incomplete And, so I toast, to what in life, matters the most. And to you mom, with glasses raised, I salute you, for all the days, you contribute to, keeping me on, the straight and narrow, just as God, has his eyes on the sparrow.

#98

"BELIEVE AND PERCEIVE"

Sometimes, words are not enough, it can, get to be rough, saying how you feel, when you want to tell, the one you are with, your love for them is real. The words you choose mean a lot, to determine, whether or not, you get your point across, it's a coin toss. When you try to convey, what you have to say, you need for them, to believe and perceive. Show sincerity, speaking with clarity.

Express yourself, to put them at ease, if you please. Stress the fact, be exact. Confess your intentions, make sure, your dialog mentions, your behavior, will be in their favor.

#99
"A MANS LIFE"

On the wings of the wind, I soar free, not restricted by the bars of captivity. My spirit is aloft in space, I fly like a bird, without a trace. Fish in the ocean, you could sooner stop, it's ever flowing motion. Imagination, is God's creation, saying otherwise, could condemn you, upon you demise. Man has given, recognition, to some power, greater than he, ever since, he came to be. For centuries, we have called on forces, beyond our control, to guide us, deliver us, excuse us, for our flaws, faults, and fallacies. There has been documentation of this for eons, I can't believe, all of it, was the work, of peons. It had to come from somewhere, or, was it just a man like me, living in despair? Different cultures, have different beliefs, rituals, and traditions, that evolved from there conditions. Even so, some foster the same ideals as others, like brothers, in their diversity. Who is right, who is wrong, should we let this, make us reluctant, or makes us strong? Are bits and pieces, of everyone correct, and none of them, absolutely perfect? They could be, completely, fabricated as well, who is to tell? There are those that say, there is life after *death, then there are those that say, once you die, there is nothing left. I would like to think, that these few years, of a man's life, is not all it appears, and maybe, we can, live twice.*

#100
"TO HAVE A DREAM"

Once upon a time, some people took a chance, many years ago, to further man's advance. They set out in a boat, to sail across the sea, looking for a place, where they could be free. They came upon a spot, we call it Plymouth Rock, they thought that this might be, a good place to stop. So they got out of the ship, and stood on solid ground, and figured this should be the place, to settle down. This is what I mean, about to have a dream, looking for something, that you have never seen, going to a place, that you have never been, hoping that the people, will please let you in, you open up your heart, and give it all you've got, to find out in due time, if you should stay or not. Here we have explores, who traveled all this way, hoping they will find themselves, a better place to stay. Free of any tyranny, from which they all have fled, praying where they find themselves, they will no live to dread. To build a better life, with much prosperity, the freedom and the joys, of both for you and me. This is what they came for, what they sought with all their might, and when it all was threatened, they took up arms to fight. But what has now become of us, the mess that we have made, to now be where we are, where we were we should have stayed. We have too much oppression, many things are just the

same, unlike where we were before, we should
let freedom reign. But that's too much to ask,
liberty, justice for all, united we stand,
divided we fall.

#101
"THE NATIONS NEWEST
GUARDIAN"

One month before, Barack Obama, the
United States, first black president, is
about to become, the next, White House
resident. He has, quite a task, before him
now, but alas, he has the brass, to pull it
off, somehow. There are a lot of people,
wishing him well, just ask around, and
you will soon tell, that all those behind
him, as he starts his administration,

congratulates him, with a standing ovation. Sure, there are those, as in any case, hoping he will fall, flat on his face. But they are a minority, when it comes to this man, watch when he swears in, there will be, only room to stand. If you plan to attend, when he takes his oath, you better get there early, because he will have the most, people ever to observe, this auspicious occasion, and all will feel privileged, no matter their persuasion. Barack Obama, you are truly, a political drama. I am immensely sure, your life's story, is being written, to immortalize, your road to glory. I can't wait to see, when it hits the big screen, what you have become, seems more like a dream. I am very impressed, you have made quite an accomplishment, and I know, history will show, that the things you said, are things you meant. Unlike many of those, who came before you, I am confident, when you speak, what you say is true. So here's looking at you kid, in a manner of speaking, the whole country is watching, waiting, and seeking, answers to solve, the problems of life, like how to avoid living in strife. We feel with you, we have a fighting chance, and can come up with ways, to improve our circumstance. So hit the ground running, full speed ahead, and know that you and yours are in our prayers, when we go to bed. May God bless you, yours, and all of us too, and allow all of us to prosper, until your term is through.

Bonus #1
"FOR GANG BANGGERS"

All you know to talk about, is Glock and Slugs, but you do not know the meaning, of being real thugs. You think you're doing something, when you battle for turf, but no one ever told you, what the corner was worth. So you make a dollar, maybe two, maybe three, but do you see now what it costs you, when you're not even free. Thinking that you're bad, trying to be a big man but you're wasting all your life, spending it in the can. When you go home, you see those you don't know, having done time, just to go with the flow. So scared of being different, you won't take a stand, how bad are you then, when you run from the man. Telling war stories, you can joke, you can play, it's by the grace of God you live to see another day. Think a gun is something, with a bullet in it, but what's a bullet going to do, to a tank when it hit. You might as well have sling shots, when you go against these, they shoot the kind of shells that can level the trees. Yes there are times, when you must go to war, but it means a whole lot, when you know what it's for. Like for the money, that's long overdue, and how about how, they still take it from you? How they do that, let me see can I say, it's a well-known fact, that they do it this way. When you're in the streets, in the cold and the rain, running out in traffic, like somebody insane, they sit back and watch you make your money you see, then they put you in a courtroom, did you think it was free? They charge you with crimes, and offer you pleas, then slap you with fines, your attorney has fees. Now all of your dough, has gone up in smoke, so much you can see, how a horse it can choke. So while you shed your blood, shed your sweat and your tears, I'll tell you about the man, and how he's dogged you for years. He puts you into places, so you can't move around, and any time he's ready, level them to the ground. Jefferson Village, that was first, now he's using Blackwell, just for quenching his thirst. He has a thirst for blood, watch him eat you can tell, he eats his meat rare, not medium well. This is the kind of enemy, you're up against, you

better know your allies, because the war
has commenced. I'm not done with you
yet, stick around if you please, stop
acting like a dog, who has been
scratching his flees. You need to hear
some things, and I will tell you the
truth, about the way the man is busy,
brainwashing the youth. He uses
television, and even magazine, a lot of
things in them, our kids have never even
seen. They lead them to believe, that's
what the world is about, but most live in
the ghetto, and they'll never leave out.
So showing them these things, don't
mean a damn thing, they will never buy
a jet, working at a Burger King. What
they need to know, about the meaning of
life, is how the rich lives off the poor,
like a head full of lice. And it doesn't

stop there, it even goes into space,
because that's the destination, of the
human race. They're working on a
station, somewhere that they can live,
and what they leave behind, this to us
they will give. Pollution, famine,
pestilence and the stink, we'll even have
the water, that you can't even drink, but
they will make their own, it's only H2O,
and if you ever went to school, this,
you would also know.

Bonus #2

"FOR GREENBAY PACKER FANS"

Welcome to our home, we call it Green Bay, Wisconsin, we come to play a game, and we play with no nonsense. In the wind and the cold, even freezing rain, when it comes to playing football, we feel no pain. If that's not enough, we have some more you know, let it snow let it snow let it snow let it snow. At Lambow Field, we will make you squeal, home of the Lambow Leap, an all you suckers weep. For all you copy cats, who ride our jockey straps, here's where it started at, and you know that. Talk about Bret, like he's over the hill, all the rest of you chumps, are just run of the mill. He's like a super star, throwing passes very far, as if he's riding in his car, or driving strokes under par. The 4 on his back, should be an S on his chest, when throwing the ball, he's never second best. Playing like a superman, amazing each and every fan, when the ball is in his hands, the seats are empty in the stands. There is no risk that he won't take like the man of steel, he should wear a cape. With the game on the line, an everything at stake, your defense will lie, in his wake. Coach Lombardy, top hats to you, we'll bring your trophy home, before our song is through. For those who doubt, and think we tease, we'll lay you out, like lumps of cream cheese. If that's not enough, one more thing, we can sing, we can sing, we can sing, we can sing.